Forks Over Knives

What Do We Learn From
Forks over Knives Documentary?

Guide to Eating Plant-based Diet

And Delicious Plant-Based Recipes

By

WaraWaran Roongruangsri

Phawana Publishing
Good Health Content

ISBN-13: 978-1530060818
ISBN-10: 1530060818

Part of the secret of success in life is to eat what you like and let the food fight it out inside.

-Mark Twain

CONTENTS

AUTHOR'S NOTE

Forks over Knives is considered one of the best books on health and nutrition. This is because it is like reading several books, but it will only take you an hour and a half to read it. What a bargain! Forks over Knives is captivating as it clearly displays the relationship between food and nutrition and teaches us how those choices affect our health in the short and long-run. Not only does this book give us a comprehensive look at our food and health, but also a detailed description.

Forks over Knives does more than present truths. It follows the lives of many people who are struggling with their health and how they practice improvement by undertaking nothing more than altering their diet. These participants established that they had lower cholesterol, blood pressure and resting heart rate, blood sugar and other ailments that America is trying to cure with pills. The people threw away much of the medication together with the rich, high-fat, sugar-loaded diet we in America have become acquainted with. The results are amazing!

In this eBook "Healthy Eating and Diet with Forks over Knives: What Do We Learn From This Book?, Guide to Healthy Eating, Diet and Lifestyle with Natural Plant-Based Foods" will offer you good information in Forks over Knives which shapes a bridge from doubt about health to the breath-taking reality, crossing the gap of misinformation enacted by the meat and dairy industries.

With this creation, and its information on eating correctly, it will walk you, step-by-step, through the process which was developed to aid people in getting all of the information they need.

In this book, you will obtain information about:
-    Forks over Knives: A Book That Will Save Your Life
-    Forks over Knives: What Will We Learn From This Film?
-    Why Change to A Plant-Based Diet?
-    How You Can Transition to a Whole Foods, Plant Based Diet
-    How to Use the Plant-Based Diet to Lose Weight

- Plant-Based Diet: And Practical Tips for Your Meal Preparation
- Forks over Knives: Plant-Based Diet Sample Recipes

Thanks for downloading the book! I am sure you will enjoy it!

Happy Reading!

WaraWaran Roongrungsri

1. FORKS OVER KNIVES: A BOOK THAT WILL SAVE YOUR LIFE

If you are not a vegan, you are killing yourself slowly with the food you are eating. You are killing yourself with the untrue beliefs that you have about the nutritional standing of animal products. You are killing yourself by generating in your body high cholesterol, hypertension and diabetes, obesity, heart disease and cancer. And, if you do not believe this, go see the documentary. It could save your life.

I promise that if you have the readiness to see this educational and entertaining documentary, you will have the essential knowledge to reverse many disease brewing in your body (as well as heart disease and cancer), get off medications you may think are essential in maintaining good health, lose weight and feel unlimited.

These aren't idle claims. This documentary shows scientific studies which were done by devoted doctors and researchers who have established the healing power of a whole food, plant diet which eliminates animal products, oils and processed foods.

We have been defrauded, by friends, by government and big business into trusting that we need the proteins in meat and calcium in milk in order to flourish. This could not be further from the truth. It is those products which destroy the endothelial cells around our blood vessels, which then leads to heart disease, death from heart attacks, and coronary bypass surgery.

The title of the documentary expresses this issue of bypass surgery in the logic that when we put on our fork foods that heal and not harm us, we can spare our self the experience of getting our chest cut open, a vein removed from our leg and sewn onto the heart to bypass the blocked up arteries which we have created by consuming an animal-based diet.

YES, YOU ARE WHAT YOU EAT

If you would like to live in denial, it best you do not see this documentary. If you would like to open your eyes to a humble solution that will save your life and the lives of the people you love, and begin to solve huge economic problems within the country, known as the health care/ pharmaceutical business, you should see this documentary.

You are well aware of the obesity epidemic in the country. Are you aware, however, aware that the current generation of children might be the first generation to live a shorter lifespan than their parents? We are finding childhood diabetes, obesity and hypertension to be like never before. This is insane! We are addicted to trash. We are killing the children with terribly toxic food habits.

Unlike "Food, Inc." another great documentary about the food that we eat, "Forks over Knives" does not probe into the terrible, cruel, brutal harshness unleashed on animals in the sardonic pursuit of gathering food sources which are killing us not only spiritually, but also literally. It is a straight-forward, methodical, clear interpretation of facts that can't be disputed. Denied, yes it can. Disputed, not a chance.

Surely, there are those people who will choose to look at the documentary through cynical eyes, and mock the vegan rebellion as an example of hippy California dreaming, nouveau silliness. Do not be one of those people. The only person you will be fooling is you.

I challenge you to learn the facts behind these foods you are eating. I challenge you to test your predispositions and fears. Go to see the film and take a first step in the direction of changing your life in amazing, exciting ways you cannot possibly imagine.

What Do We Learn From Forks over Knives documentary?

2. FORKS OVER KNIVES: WHAT WILL WE LEARN FROM THIS FILM?

Consider that heart disease, stroke, diabetes, cancer and obesity are among the most serious health-related complications which cause the deaths of masses of Americans almost every year. At least one individual in USA is killed due to heart disease every minute. At least 1500 people every day die from cancer-related illness. Combined, heart disease and/or cancer will kill one million Americans each year.

One third of the children born today may cultivate diabetes in their lifetime. Two thirds of Americans are overweight, and half of them are taking a form of prescribed drugs. These are very astonishing statistics, right?

In fact, surprisingly, the health of Americans is

deteriorating year after year with mounting incidences of renewing diseases despite having the most advanced medical accommodations in the world.

FORKS OVER KNIVES is a film that displays the idea that if you discard processed and animal-based foods and remedy to a plant-based diet, the mainstream of severe and fatal diseases can and will be prevented, handled and reversed.

The name itself, "FORKS OVER KNIVES", specifies using a fork instead of going under the knife (surgery). The documentary delivers an eye-opening vision into the studies of nutritional researchers and well-known doctors who suggest that animal products and/or processed foods contribute to almost every disease. However, whole-food, plant-based diets can significantly reduce and reverse many crippling health conditions.

This film also reveals the remarkable journeys of two resourceful researchers, Dr. T. Colin Campbell and Dr. Caldwell Esselstyn.

Dr. Colin Campbell was raised on a farm. His family lived on milk from dairy-product cows. Ultimately, he recognized the damaging effects of animal-based food and striking healing power of plant-based foods. He also corresponds that plants, such as grains, will substitute the need for protein in the human body.

Dr. Campbell decided to conduct a series of tests on lab mice in order to determine the effect of casein (the main protein in dairy). In one of his experiments, he kept the mice in one group and swapped their diets back and forth between 5% and then 20% dairy protein in three week recesses.

The results revealed a straight link among animal protein and cancer growth. When the rats were fed 20% protein, premature liver tumor growth exploded. After, whenever the mice were given 5% protein, tumor growth decreased. This was an indication that the cancer growth could be turned on and off by regulating the level intake of bad proteins.

Dr. Caldwell Esselstyne revealed some startling statistics. In 1978, the odds of a woman receiving breast cancer in Kenya was eighty-two times lower than that in the USA. In Japan, in 1958, only eighteen people died of prostate cancer, whereas the disease killed 14,000 people in USA, even though the population of the USA was only twice as much as Japan.

Other critical information is included in this film which indicates an inspirational notion that a whole-food, plant-based diet is definitely the answer to a healthier, disease-free life.

The documentary shadows the inspirational stories of numerous normal men and women embracing whole-food, plant based diets in order to treat their crippling health conditions by getting completely off their daily medications. It will inspire you to progress towards becoming an action-taker, leading a long and healthy life.

3. WHY CHANGE TO A PLANT-BASED DIET?

Contrary to what people are taught about nourishment in all cultures, the mainstream are kept in the dark concerning what the best diet for us is. This is not shocking when you understand that governments provide us with nutritional guidelines, the same governments who are connected with powerful organizations such as meat, dairy, and egg industries, who expect and demand that their products be promoted in their dietary guidelines. Our culture and traditions also keep us glued to habits and unhealthy behaviors.

Advanced Lipoprotein Fingerprinting is a precise cholesterol test which allows doctors to recognize health risks which traditional screens can miss. This process separates lipids in our blood to create a thorough cholesterol profile helping doctors to identify patients who are at risk for heart disease. The comprehensive graph permits a doctor to accurately analyze a patient's complete risk profile and display the effectiveness of a diet or treatment routine.

This forward-thinking diagnostic technique can help doctors diagnose initial warning signs for coronary heart disease, which does kill more than 2,600 Americans each day, according to the American Heart Association. High LDL cholesterol is a main cause of coronary heart disease, according to the National Cholesterol Education Program.

LipidLabs advanced the Advanced Lipoprotein Fingerprinting Process and the outcomes decipher to more precise and exact data in which to make clinical decisions and monitor patient therapy and prevention at sensible costs.

Heart disease is a number one killer of men and women in the United States. This makes sense when you recognize some rudimentary principles about nutrition.

- Cholesterol in the diet comes from animal foods.
- The human body will produce all the cholesterol it really needs.
- The majority of saturated fat in our diet comes from animal food.

- All that the human body needs for outstanding health can be found in plant-based food.
- The main fuel that the body uses for energy: carbohydrates/simple sugars.
- Too much protein has been linked with kidney problems.
- Eating a diet mostly rich in animal foods is linked with heart disease, cancers - including breast cancer and prostate cancer, stroke, diabetes, and many other life-taking diseases.

5 Great Benefits to Get From a Plant-Based Diet

A plant-based diet contains a great percentage of food obtained from plants as opposed to animals. This means eating nuts - whole grains – lentils – peas – beans – fruits - and vegetables. Nonetheless, this style of dieting does not need to be firmly vegetarian. Here are five health benefits that come from eating plant foods:

Blood pressure

A plant-based diet suggests a seamless source of potassium-rich foods and can help to naturally lower your blood pressure. Fruits and vegetables as well as seeds – nuts – legumes -and whole grain include sufficient amounts of vitamin B6 and potassium for strong blood pressure. Animal foods, like meat, include nominal potassium and lead to high cholesterol and blood pressure.

Cholesterol

A noteworthy benefit of implementing a plant-based diet is the capability of lowering your cholesterol. Plants remain cholesterol-free, even the most saturated kinds like cacao and coconut. For this purpose, eating a diet that regularly consists of plant-based foods will offer a simple answer to dropping cholesterol. Wonderful food choices will lower the rates of heart disease and cholesterol including seeds – nuts - whole grains – fruits - and vegetables.

Blood Sugar

A very effective technique to regulate high blood sugar is increasing fiber in your diet. A fiber-rich diet is seamless in helping to slow the absorption of sugar in your bloodstream. An additional benefit would be the capability of controlling hunger throughout the day. Also, fiber will help to balance the levels of cortisol in your blood stream, which is accountable for your feelings of stress. Many animal foods have a noteworthy hand in increasing your blood sugar level.

Cancer

A plant-based diet which includes low-fat, whole foods are the most efficient choices for facilitating the

WaraWaran Roongrungsri

risk of cancer. Certain cancers, like breast and colon cancer are at higher risk for those who eat a diet mostly containing animal foods.

Weight Loss

A diet containing plant-based and whole foods, having minimal processed sugars and low fat, is sure to help with losing weight. Another benefit comes from a diet that is great in clean, raw whole foods. Weight loss is certainly going to occur when your daily diet includes a greater percentage of vitamins and minerals, and fiber compared with proteins and animal fats. A well-organized plant-based diet has potential to help you lose 4-6 pounds within two weeks. This will also guarantee you are not left feeling hungry.

Eating a diet built on whole, plant-based foods will reduce your risk of a wide-ranging gamut of diseases, including heart disease, obesity, diabetes, and cancer. What we should be eating is our chief concern. Why does a whole-food, plant-based diet deliver optimum nutrition? Click here to get the answers to these questions in detail.

4. HOW YOU CAN TRANSITION TO A WHOLE FOODS, PLANT BASED DIET

If you are changing the way you eat on an everyday basis, you have to be realistic with your approach. You can't assume you must stop eating the foods you enjoy cold turkey, as that will not do anything but add additional weight to your body when you crash from the emotional removal of it. How you can transition to a whole foods, plant based diet isn't as perplexing as it seems at first. It will just necessitate focus and will power initially.

A plant-based diet is clearly one that doesn't allow cupcakes or doughnuts. You are encouraged to consume foods that are natural. Organic is the top choice to go with when changing to a plant- based diet. You will have to purchase your food for the weeks forward so you will have plenty of choices when you look for a snack. This will discourage you from misplacing vision of the diet and cheating by taking the first thing you see in your food closet. Be sure to clean out all the food that is presently in your home/office that is not in your plant-based diet, and substitute it with healthier choices as.

You will want to produce meals for your plant-based diet which are rich in antioxidants. You should get a book and/or follow a plan on the internet which you can access for free and obtain great tips/ideas for meals and snacks which will guide you through the course. There are a few other tricks which can help you changeover into a plant-based diet. The most important one being to prepare your mind.

Mental awareness is vital in planning a huge life change such as this in changing the whole way you will eat. You have to realize that what you eat should be a matter of giving your body enough energy to get through the activities you participate during the day. Food is not about cheesecake or pasta. It is what you need mentally and physically, and the foods that cause temptation to cheat on your plant-based diet are simply to satisfy your mind, because your body doesn't need those empty calories. After you have been on the plant-based diet for a while, you will begin to notice your body is no longer craving the fatty foods. Check out cookbooks that will provide added recipes and snack ideas. A blender/food processor will help in getting the vegetables in that you need. Experiment with diverse food textures and groupings until you find some that you like. Prepare your own juice and dishes with fresh ingredients for your diet success!

5. HOW TO USE THE PLANT-BASED DIET TO LOSE WEIGHT

I am a strong believer that great health and long-term health management is deep-rooted in nutrition and a balanced, well-chosen food group, together with a consistent exercise regimen. Weight loss, weight management, and good health will all come together. Once I had this undoubtedly implanted in my brain, I then realized that the foundation of this rational was really very simple.

Eat fresh food, generally plants. I am not promoting a vegetarian diet, as I myself am not an active vegetarian. I do think, however, that a well-thought out and accomplished vegetarian diet can be good for weight loss and exceptional health.

When I say to eat fresh food, it is just that simple. You must stay away from factory-made, extremely processed foods. If you put thought into why there are out-of-control obesity epidemics in the United States, and you then put two and two together, you would realize that this is entrenched into two factors, a huge lack of fresh food, sedentary lifestyles and little to no exercise at all.

The plant-based diet is not only about eating plants, fruits and vegetables. It Includes fish, chicken, and additional meats, only if you want to eat meat, and the key is moderation.

You should eat at least 80 % plant-based diet. Most foods, such as nuts – grains – beans - sweet potatoes etc., are plant-based foods.

You get all the nutrition and enzymes you need from the plant-based foods that you eat. Also, when you overcook vegetables, you lose an abundance of nutrition and then you eliminate the valuable enzymes. Together with lightly-cooked vegetables, you should also eat fruits and raw vegetables every day. Salads are awesome but you should also consider creating a green drink. Here is a simple recipe that I make almost every day. Use a blender, a Vita Mix or other. Add a handful of kale, a little bit of fresh parsley, one sprig of celery, a small bit of cabbage, one/two cored apples, one/two cored pears, and a wedge of lemon with the peel. Add in more than one apple or pear depending on how sweet you like it.

You can also mess around with diverse fruits, like berries and blueberries. This drink does not taste like it looks. The fruit and the vegetables together provides a pleasant taste. The idea is to receive a healthy shot of fresh vegetables and fruit, with a low-caloric content and tons of nutritional/antioxidant content and fiber. This is a fantastic, healthy, and fresh plant-based weight loss drink.

Losing weight and/or getting healthy is really about altering your food awareness, eating a pure diet. Meaning that the food you eat has not gone through manufacturing or processing. The grains you eat aren't refined. You should select brown rice as opposed to white rice, whole grain pasta (occasionally) and sweet potatoes rather than regular white potatoes. The idea is to avoid foods that instantly turn into sugar inside your system.

When you eat meats and/or fish, eat smaller portions and also avoid rich sauces, large amounts of butter or dairy-based condiments. For adding taste to cooked food you, use herbs, garlic, coconut oil/virgin olive oil and also grape seed oil is fine. Stay away from other oils. Do not over eat dairy products, buy almond milk rather than cow milk, and limit cheeses and butter. Consider yogurt as opposed to cream when cooking, and be sure to stay clear of refined sugars.

Beware of food-like substances, such as high fructose corn syrup, trans fats, hydrogenated oil, high amounts of sugar, high amounts of salt, tons of preservatives and chemicals. They are the culprits that are in the processed, refined and boxed foods in the mainstream market.

Begin by changing when you eat. Eat smaller meals more often, and do not eat meals after 4 or 5 P.M. If you would like a snack later on, eat fruit. It is good to take a walk after your last meal. Sitting on the couch after and then going to bed will put on the weight and keep it on.

This concept to become a conscious eater is at the heart of losing the weight and being in great health. It may be a huge change for you as habits are the hardest part of our lives to change. Take it one step at a time and continue to stay focused, put lots of time into it, educate yourself, and it will be well worth it.

6. PLANT-BASED DIET: AND PRACTICAL TIPS FOR YOUR MEAL PREPARATION

Plant-based meal preparation is not difficult but it will take time. Here is how you can go through the procedure of making sure meal planning does not become a burden on your time or your taste buds.

First

You need to make a list of foods that you already have at your home in your refrigerator/pantry (excepting dry goods.)

Second

You should think of the kinds of meals you would like to prepare. You can choose amongst the following:

- Breakfast - porridges (including oatmeal, millet, quinoa, buckwheat and rice), smoothies and some pancakes.
- Snacks - bread, muffins, cookies, vegetables (raw) (carrots, red bell peppers and cauliflower), seasonal fruit, nuts and seeds.
- Lunches and Dinners - soup, stew, salad, pasta, risotto, curries, tortillas, steamed vegetables with boiled grains and legumes.
- Desserts - berries, muffin, cookie, brownie, ice cream, pudding made of avocado or banana, dark chocolate, applesauce with dried fruit and raw buckwheat cream.

When you are meal planning, please remember to:

- Have a variation of food each day - different grains, legumes, vegetables, fruits, nuts and seeds.
- Eat a rainbow every day - something green, yellow, orange, purple, red and white/brown.
- Choose between the seasonal fruits/vegetables in your region. These will cost less and are freshest.
- If you happened to have a grain-based breakfast, you will want to have fruits or

vegetables with nuts for your mid-morning snack.

- If you happened to have a smoothie for breakfast, then have porridge, a muffin, a cookies or bread for your mid-morning snack.

- If you want a grain-based dessert (muffins or cookies), have less grains with dinner or don't have them at all.

- Be sure to have at least a tablespoon of ground flax seeds or chia seeds each day to gets enough omega 3s.

- Always have handy nuts or seeds and vegetables/fruits rich in carotenoids (such as carrots, sweet potatoes, leafy greens, like spinach and kale, romaine lettuce, squash, cantaloupe melons, red bell peppers, apricots, peas, broccoli, tomatoes) because the fat helps to absorb vitamins.

Third

Draw a table the equivalent of seven days or the number of days you are designing your meal plan for.

Fill in breakfasts with choices such as grains and/or smoothies.

When you are done, proceed to Step 2 and choose specific grains, fruits and vegetables for your smoothies, depending upon what you have and on seasonality with variety in mind.

After you are good at the first stage, skip it and jump right to Step 2.

You do not need to consume different smoothies all the time. For example, during orange season, my family had orange smoothies for a few months in a row. We sweetened them with bananas, carrots or mangos and always made sure we added greens.

After breakfast, plan your lunch and dinner. Use the identical steps you used with your breakfast meals. Put in choices like soup – risotto – pasta – curry, etc. If you have lunch in a café or buffet, you won't have as much planning for those meals. For supper, cook every other day enabling you to eat leftovers every other night.

If you take lunch with you or eat at home, leave the leftovers for the next day at lunch.

Now, begin thinking about recipes to make. Use vegetables you have at home on your first day or two (think of seasonality/variety.)

When you have used up what you have at home, choose different vegetables of different colors for meals in the next few days.

Snacks: Mid-Morning and Afternoon

Keep in mind: if you did have a grain-based breakfast, you should have some fruits or vegetables with nuts for your mid-morning snack. If you did have fruits in the a.m., have vegetables in the afternoon. Begin by filling in the snack rows with choices such as raw vegetables, nuts, fruits, and grains.

It is worth reiterating to consider using what you have in stock and the veggies and fruits you are going to use in the morning smoothies and main meals. Also, be sure to keep seasonality in mind and eat a rainbow each day.

Tip: It would be wise to bake a big batch of muffins, cookies and bread to freeze for the week and have on hand for snacks.

Desserts!

There are people who do not want dessert after dinner, but I think they are in the minority.

Deciding what you will have for dessert hinges on how substantial your menu has been for that day. For example, let's say you had coconut curry, then do not have a rich dessert that contains nuts or avocado. In its place, have berries, banana pudding or ice cream.

If you did not have grains, eat one or two oil-free,

sugar-free muffins as dessert.

Fourth

Planning is creating your shopping list allowing for what is on your menu. You may shop every day or once for the week - whichever is easier.

Leftovers

If you have leftovers at the week's end, use them first the next week.

You can use leftover vegetables as snacks because there is no harm in eating veggies.

Sometimes we have half a banana or avocado left over, or half a can beans or crushed tomatoes. If you do, alter your plan accordingly. For instance, use those leftovers (onions, celery, tomatoes) in lunch/dinner recipes.

It is not necessary to use everything right away. Some items keep well like celery, cans of beans, lentils and dry goods.

> Tip: To avoid leftovers, assemble a shopping list prior to adding snacks and desserts. First, use items left over from breakfast and main meals for snack and dessert prior to adding new ideas.

7. FORKS OVER KNIVES: PLANT-BASED DIET SAMPLE RECIPES

Egyptian Breakfast Beans (Full Me dames)

Ingredients

1½ pounds dry fava beans, soak for

8 - 10 hours

1 med. yellow onion, peeled and diced - small

4 cloves of garlic, peeled and minced

1 tsp ground cumin

zest and juice from 1 lemon

Sea Salt

1 lemon, quartered

Instructions

1. Drain and rinse beans and put them into a large pot. Cover with four inches water and bring to boil on high heat. Decrease to medium heat, cover, and cook till tender, 1½ to 2 hours.
2. While beans are cooking, panfry onion in medium skillet/saucepan on medium heat for 8 to 10 min., or until tender and beginning to brown. Add garlic, cumin, lemon zest and juice and cook 5 min. longer. Set aside.
3. When beans are cooked, drain all but ½ cup of liquid from pot and add onion mixture to beans. Mix and season with salt. Serve garnished with lemon.

Crispy Baked Falafels

Ingredients

2 (15-ounce) cans of chickpeas, drained/rinsed

1 med. yellow onion, chopped

6 cloves of garlic, chopped

4 tbsp. fresh parsley, chopped

1 tbsp. arrowroot powder

4 tsp. ground coriander

2 tsp. ground cumin

Sea salt & black pepper, for taste

Instructions

1. Preheat oven to 400°F.
2. Put all ingredients in a food processor and mix, leaving texture to the beans.
3. Shape into balls using an ice cream scoop or tablespoon. Place on a nonstick baking sheet, bake for 25 minutes.

Roasted Vegetable Pasta

Ingredients

1 lb. pasta

1/2 red onion, sliced

2 med. carrots, cut like thin matchsticks

1 pint small tomatoes, cut in half

1 med. zucchini, cut like thin matchsticks

1 lb. eggplant, skin on, cut in cubes

1/4 tsp. salt

2 1/2 tsp. chopped thyme leaves

3 cloves of garlic, minced

2 tbsp. lemon juice

3 tbsp. balsamic vinegar

1/2 tsp. red pepper flakes (optional)

Instructions

1. Cook pasta according to directions. Drain, pour back into pot.
2. Preheat oven - 425°F. Get two large Silicone or non-stick baking sheets.
3. In large bowl, put in red onion – carrots – tomatoes – zucchini – eggplant - and salt. Mix together. Spread on baking sheets and put into oven.
4. Roast for about 20 minutes, take out, add thyme – garlic - and lemon juice, stir, and throw back in oven until veggies begin looking browned around edges, 10 to 15 minutes.
5. Add roasted vegetables to cooked pasta, pour in balsamic vinegar, pepper flakes, pinch of salt and pepper, & stir. Taste - add more garlic – vinegar - lemon juice -

and thyme. If you want more greens, serve
hot pasta on bed of arugula or spinach
adding a bit of lemon juice. Done.

Chickpea Omelet

Ingredients

1 cup of chickpea flour

½ tsp. onion powder

½ tsp. garlic powder

¼ tsp. white pepper

¼ tsp. black pepper

1/3 cup of nutritional yeast

½ tsp. baking soda

3 green onions (white and green part),
chopped

4 ounces of sautéed mushrooms (optional)

Instructions

1. Combine chickpea flour, the onion
    powder, the garlic powder, the white
    pepper, the black pepper, the nutritional

yeast, and the baking soda in small bowl. Add one cup of water and stir until batter is smooth.

2.   Heat frying pan on medium heat. Pour batter into pan, like you are making pancakes. Sprinkle one to two tablespoons green onion and mushroom into batter for each omelet. Flip omelet. When the underneath is brown, flip omelet again, and cook other side for about a minute.

3.   Serve this amazing chickpea omelet topped with tomatoes – spinach – salsa - hot sauce - or whatever plant-perfect fixings you would like.

Hollywood Bowl ---- Brown Rice Salad

Ingredients

1 cup of brown rice

1 zucchini, chopped fine (approximately 1 cup)

1 cucumber, chopped fine (approximately 1 cup)

2 tomatoes, chopped fine (approximately 1 cup)

1/2 cup chopped green onions (fine), (white

and light green parts)

1 cup of chopped cilantro leaves

3 to 4 tbsp. fresh lemon juice (about 2 lemons)

1/4 tsp. fresh ground black pepper

Sea Salt

Instructions

1. Rinse rice, and place in saucepan with 2 cups of water. Bring water to boil on high heat. Reduce heat to low and cover. Simmer until rice is tender, approximately 45 minutes.
2. Remove pan from heat and let it stand, covered, for about 10 - 15 minutes.
3. Transfer rice to large bowl, and let cool for few minutes or until no longer steaming.
4. Add zucchini – cucumber – tomatoes - green onions - cilantro, 3 tbsp. lemon juice, pepper & salt to taste. Mix well. Take a taste and you can add more lemon juice if needed.
5. Cover and chill, let stand at room temperature for at least 30 minutes, to allow the flavors to meld together.

6. Taste & adjust seasonings. Serve cold or room temperature. Store in airtight container in the refrigerator for two to three days.

Chocolate Chia Pudding

Ingredients

1 cup of unsweetened and unflavored or chocolate plant milk

½ cup of (packed) pitted dates, + another 1 to 3 dates

3 tbsp. chia seeds

1½ tbsp. of cocoa powder

⅛ tsp. sea salt (rounded)

½ tsp. vanilla extract (pure)

2 to 3 tbsp. unsweetened shredded coconut (which is optional)

2 tbsp. mini (nondairy) chocolate chips (optional, but tasty)

Instructions

1. Put milk - dates - chia seeds – cocoa – salt - and vanilla in blender, puree for a minute or so (depending on blender), until seeds are ground. Taste, if you would like it sweeter, add a few more dates.

2. Transfer mixture to large bowl, stir in coconut and chocolate chips (if you are using), and refrigerate it until chilled, ½ hour or so. (Will thicken with chilling but can be eaten right away.)

3. Serve, sprinkle with coconut, if wanted, and top with berries or any other fruit, if wanted.

Pumpkin Pie Squares

Ingredients

10 dates, pitted & diced (approximately 1 cup diced)

1½ cups of oat flour

2 tsp. pumpkin pie spice (see notes)

1 15-ounce can of cooked pumpkin (and not pumpkin pie mix)

1 tsp. vanilla extract

½ cup of unsweetened, unflavored - plant

milk

1 cup of Macadamia Vanilla Frosting

Instructions

1. Soak dates in a bowl with ¾ cup of water for about 15 minutes.
2. Preheat oven to 375°F.
3. Place flour and pumpkin pie spice in large bowl. Place soaked dates, date-soaked water (see "texture" notes), vanilla and milk in blender and purée until smooth (1 - 2 minutes). Pour mixture into bowl of flour and spice, add pumpkin, and mix with wooden spoon until the dry ingredients are combined.
4. Scrape batter onto an 8 × 8 inch parchment-lined baking sheet (or a nonstick baking pan). Cook 25 - 30 minutes on 375°F, until lightly brown with a few cracks on top. Let cool for about 10 to 15 minutes before serving.
5. Scrape batter into an 8 × 8 inch parchment-lined baking sheet (or a nonstick baking pan). Cook for about 25 to 30 minutes on 375°F, until lightly brown with a few cracks on top. Let cool for at least 10 - 15 minutes before cutting.

6. If preferred, top with Macadamia Vanilla Frosting right before serving, or use rotary cheese grater to dust a little lightly with grated macadamia or other nuts. Store in refrigerator overnight allowing to firm up squares, then you can pack in a lunch or pack as a snack.

Printed in Great Britain
by Amazon

12187167R00031